C H ⋯ S

of

DELIGHT

CHANNELS
of
DELIGHT

DANIEL L. FRENCH

XULON PRESS

Xulon Press
2301 Lucien Way #415
Maitland, FL 32751
407.339.4217
www.xulonpress.com

Paperback ISBN-13: 978-1-66284-311-2
Ebook ISBN-13: 978-1-66284-312-9

TABLE OF CONTENTS

DEDICATION. VII

FORWARD. IX

ALL CAKED UP. XI

INTRODUCTION. XV

THIS BOOK IS NOT ABOUT GOLF – REALLY. 1

DEALING WITH ISSUES OF MILITARY SERVICE. 6

DEALING WITH THE CHALLENGES OF LIFE. 10

DEALING WITH CHALLENGES OF BEING OLD. 28

REMEMBERING THE LONG-TERM CAREGIVERS. . . . 34

DEALING WITH THE ISSUES OF DEATH. 37

THE MOST PERSONAL OF ALL MY WRITINGS. 42

DEALING WITH BUSINESS ISSUES. 46

GOOD, ALL OF THAT IS OVER
   NOW, I FEEL MUCH BETTER. 57

OH, "LOOKIE," BOY HAS MY LIFE CHANGED. 59

FRONT PORCH PERSPECTIVES. 74

I DID COME BACK. 77

DEALING WITH THE LOSS OF MY LOVED ONES. . . 81

GOD'S AMAZING BLESSING. 87

THE MYSTERIOUS WAYS OF GOD. 90

ERRORS AND OMISSIONS. 115

DEDICATED TO
MY PARENTS

Albert and Ruth French

Times within a past, gone like a gentle breeze,
Faded Photographs, Rusty Memories.
Where are they now? With their
hope for love and life.
Could they soon be us? Can we
profit from their strife?

Setting a stage for life, planting a seed of faith.
Building a future for all, with much care, devotion
and grace.
Where are they now? These flowers from the past.
Rusty Memories, Faded Photographs

Son, Danny

FOREWORD

I've never been accused of having the deepest mind in town. Oh, I can hold my own in a conversation. Although now my hearing is bad, and I sometimes miss a few of the things said.

This little publication is a result of nearly a life-time of writing. Sometimes, when I'm in the mood, I can say some creative things.

Coming up with a title took me some time (told you, I'm not quick), then I remembered what was said in my senior year high school annual. I never made the "most likely to do" anything list. So, I guess I didn't "remember" anything. However, under my picture was the statement "Channels of Delight."

Not quite sure what that means, but I have always tried to approach each day of my life with wonder and delight.

So in fulfilling my classmate's (whoever you are) description of me, and looking at what I've been writing over the years, I can see many "channels of delight." Think upon this as a transistor radio; turn the page, turn the channel.

   Hopefully one or two of these "channels" delights you, the reader.

ALL CAKED UP

———◆———

The other day, my computer quit. By some quark of fate (not my fault) it froze up. Wouldn't move. Just stopped doing what it was doing. After a few verbal outbursts (nothing dirty) and some major keyboard shenanigans, I finally figured out how to exit the program and turn the thing off. All good computer people know the three simple keystrokes: Control-Alt-Delete ... pull the plug! I then followed the proper steps to get things back to normal. That was when I discovered the computer would not boot up. No matter what I did, it did nothing.

Knowing they could probably help, I approached every computer genius I knew. There was even a celebrity Microsoft employee visiting me at the time. None of them could figure out my difficulty. Finally, I called in the ultimate problem solver: my son, the computer consultant. He eventually arrived and, just like the other, was unable to fix my computer.

Now let me interject what this computer means to me. Over the years, I've created many articles, pamphlets, brochures, stories, poetry, conferences, and golf tournament publications using this specific computer. A lot of innovative and creative hard work was in its memory. It was my brains, my idea vault, and my left-hand friend.

The day after the computer went to the shop, I was told things didn't look too good. In fact, they said each time they tried to do something to the computer, the poor thing got worse. Its memory was going fast. They didn't hold out much hope for my friend.

As of this writing, I'm not sure how much, if any, of my years of computer work will be saved. For a while, I was fit to be tied. *How could this happen to me!* I wondered. *Why! Why! Why!*

Then I looked around my office and had a second thought. My office consists of items and memorabilia reflecting years of work. (By the way I charge admission for tours of my office.) In fact, my office is so loaded down with "stuff" that my desk and even the walls are barely visible. Comfortable for me, yes, but sometimes a little too much cacophony ("clutter" is too weak of a word) for certain visitors.

I then realized that my computer also had so much "stuff" in it that it had become bulky to use. There were times when I spent so much effort trying to remember where some great idea was that I failed to consider new potential. Although my computer's untimely demise was forced upon me to some degree, I'm now glad that the computer died and took all of my "great" old ideas to computer heaven. I am now forced to start anew with a fresh, uncluttered look upon my creative thinking.

Mark Twain wrote: "Every once in a while, we need to take our brain out and stomp on it, it gets all caked up." Now I realize what he meant. I was so reliant upon the past that it became more and more difficult to create the new. I've decided to look at other parts of my life and see if I'm dragging around too much "stuff" there too. Looks like I will begin building a new pile of "stuff" beginning today.

-Dan French

Introduction

Welcome to a perfect publication ...

This, I promise, is a perfect book.

Perfect in nearly every way ... except for the occasional misspelled word ... except for some transposed numbers ... except for a little typo here and a smaller typo there ... except for some bad English here and an extra preposition there ... except for minor details ... this book is *perfect* in nearly every way.

After all, if my wife doesn't find anything messed up, then this publication is perfection personified.

If, on the other hand, you find what you consider a "glaring error," then maybe I wanted it that way. I may have preferred those numbers be in that order! Anyway, if that "N" looks better than that "O" beside that "T," there's no error. I can put words any place I want. After all, most is poetry!

Anyway, no matter what you say, I will still have a perfect publication. Frustrating maybe, but still perfect.

Dan French,
Director of Error Avoidance

This Book Is Not About Golf ... *Really!*

Sometimes, your mind is not on the game ...

Played Golf Today

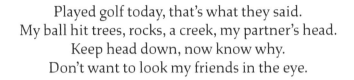

Played golf today, that's what they said.
My ball hit trees, rocks, a creek, my partner's head.
Keep head down, now know why.
Don't want to look my friends in the eye.

Played golf today, didn't play good.
Forgot the part that requires the wood,
to hit the ball and make it go.
Really didn't seem to mind it, though.

Played golf today, already forgot why.
Couldn't see the ball, moisture in the eye.
More than golf became apparent,
with each new swing, the ball went aberrant.

Played golf today, truly didn't care.
Mind kept wandering far away from there.
Missed some shots when I thought about you,
other things I'd rather do.

Sometimes, your mind is on the game ...

A Friendly Game

As I got ready to hit the ball,
A snicker and I could not decide at all
if the rumble and roar was about my stance,
or did I have a hole in my pants?

Snickers and grins can be distracting
when standing at the tee, there is no more acting.
When it comes to really hitting that orb,
it's down the middle, or the mistakes you absorb.

Funny thing happens whenever you go out,
and everyone there is talking about
the strokes they've made, the way they played.
Maybe you should come back another day.

Once on the course, you quickly find
your friends, your neighbors, those golfers sublime,
may talk a big talk, but under it all,
like you, have no idea how to hit that little ball.

So, enjoy yourself as much as you can.
Fear not the woods, the wedge, or man.
Even though there is nothing more sore
than watching a fellow golfer shoot a lower score.

You try hard, and someday you'll learn
there are things that maybe you should just spurn.
Others may joke, but remember one thing,
only one out of a hundred can play this dumb game.
Sometimes, the game stimulates your thinking ...

Golf Ball Follies

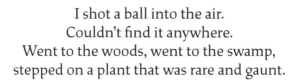

I shot a ball into the air.
Couldn't find it anywhere.
Went to the woods, went to the swamp,
stepped on a plant that was rare and gaunt.

I shot a ball, straight and narrow.
It must have landed in a hole or a furrow.
Looked right and left as I walked the grass.
Lost another ball, *what's happening?* I ask.

I shot a third ball that was lively and quick.
Hit something solid, made me feel sick.
Saw a bear fall, or was it a golfer?
Didn't find that ball, even though a prayer I offered

I shot another ball, sun in the face.
Heard it hit but couldn't embrace
the spot or the place where finally it landed.
Maybe I should take the hint I was handed.

Hit a ball, watched it curve
into a lake where the fish it disturbed.
Too deep to find, no time for a swim.
Let it go, an idea begins.

Golf is fun or so they say.
Really don't know, the way I play.
Some are happy, this I know.
Titleist, Maxflight they're making the dough.

Lost another ball, but now I feel fine.
Let it lay lost, no whimper or whine.
Now I'm happy because each time that I play,
my thirty shares of Nike doubles that day.

Dealing with Issues of Military Service...

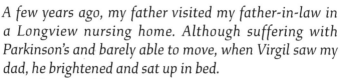

A few years ago, my father visited my father-in-law in a Longview nursing home. Although suffering with Parkinson's and barely able to move, when Virgil saw my dad, he brightened and sat up in bed.

Then the two, old gentlemen hugged. As they embraced, I realized there was more between them than mere friendship. There was something only those who have lived in harm's way could understand.

During World War II, Dad served in the South Pacific, and Virgil served in Europe. When I saw those two old soldiers together, I cried. Theirs was a comradeship that only a veteran could understand. And so I wrote this lyric for Virgil and Dad who loved their God, their country, and their family. These old soldiers' faith never faulted, nor did they ever complain.

The Old Vet

He lay there with a fuzzy brain.
With people all around, he wouldn't complain.
Knew more than they about the world he'd known.
Still smelled the powder, still felt loneliness
from home.

Three score years before, as fresh as yesterday,
He was young, and war was never meant to play
so much in his life, to steal him from his youth.
Still feels the heat of cold steel and soggy
hiking boots.

Understands an honor that only soldiers know.
A kinship, a brotherhood that only seems to grow
with age and failing bodies and slower mind
reactions.
Still tastes the acid smoke, Spam, ham-n-pea
C-rations.

There, lying in his bed, only memories left,
no one grasped his sacrifice, but those who gave
their best.
A salute to another soldier is all that we can do,
who form ranks for him, to honor what he's
been through.

He's now a fallen comrade, just like so many others.
He held his banner high, but if he had his druthers,
He'd still be on the battlefield, waiting with
his friends

with high anticipation for new orders to come in.

Their final muster called; they've joined the ranks
of heaven.
A final hill was crossed as my final salute was given.
A sound of graveside taps should cause us all
to remember
there's more to a Veteran's life then he will ever
surrender.

Dedicated to Corporal Virgil Stone,
US Army and
Corporal Layne French,
US Army Air Corps
Written by Sergeant Daniel French
US Air Force

Bought A Vietnam Veteran's Hat Today

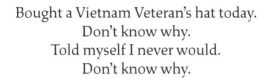

Bought a Vietnam Veteran's hat today.
Don't know why.
Told myself I never would.
Don't know why.

Never felt it necessary to flaunt what I'd
been through.
Embarrassed when people ask?
Not really. Just hard to explain.
Been there, done that, is about all I can say.

Talk with another veteran; sure, easy.
Talk to someone who doesn't know; difficult, hard.
Smells, Sights, Experiences, Excitement, Loneliness.
Can't explain feelings they would never understand.

Won't wear the hat to too many places,
don't want to cause a stir.
Could it be I'm getting older?
Bought a Vietnam Veteran's Hat today.

June 04

Consider the Apple, Consider Your Life

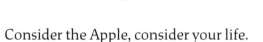

Consider the Apple, consider your life.
Not much difference, not even the strife.
You both began with God's purpose in mind.
With ending results, not readily defined.

You blossom forth with fragrance and promise.
Bursting with hope and a newfound fondness
that bees and photographers find alluring.
A mixture of love and sweetness enduring.

When at the beginning, a mere green bud,
hard and sour, just out of the mud.
Warmth and rain, love, and the Son
cradled your growth and made you THE one.

At the peak of your freshness, your moment of strife,
a cold snap happens, the meaning of life.
Now you are sweet, your juices are freed.
Time for a harvest, it is now giving you need.

At this moment, to fulfill your call
you must be willing to give up your all.
Be it effort, hard work, diligence, or faith,
your purpose for living, for rewards, you may take.

Are you that Apple that gives of this life?
Who sweetened with age and overcame strife?
Or are you the one who failed to show

your full potential, your reason to grow?
While there's time, decide, or you will be
old and wrinkled and still on that tree.

January 99

Fleeting Moments

———————•———————

A Father's hands, though rough or soft,
should be strong and used with care.
A fleeting moment is all we have.
Our dreams, our life, our hopes to share.

Little hands of trust are those
whose future we've been given to boast.
A fleeting moment is all we have
with the ones who should mean the most.

Tender hands of trust are those
who, beside us, travel through life.
A fleeting moment is all we have
to honor God's gift of a wife.

Wrinkled hands of the aged are those
who remember their time of youth.
A fleeting moment is all we have
to accept God's eternal truth.

God's plan for man is not to build
with wood or steel or straw.
A fleeting moment is all we have
to build that which will never fall.

May 95

Family Reunion

Not enough hours in the day, as we often say.
Before we know it, living life allows
time to slip away.

With sudden scorn, days are months,
and months turn to years.
Time is mapped with sorrow and heartache and
laughter and sometimes cheers.

Elders pass, and children grow.
The numbness of our life flows.
Has it been that long? we ask.
Oh, where does my time go?

Not every chance to gather is taken.
"We'll see them next time around."
But life goes on, and reality mounts,
and our *"next"* is never found.

A chance like now comes only once,
when we can all be here.
So enjoy the moment, enjoy the instant,
enjoy those stories you hear.

Seems our family still survives in name,
although many will surely belabor
that some are French, some are Ballard,
but all are proudly Tabor.
(I couldn't get Groseclose or Hodock to rhyme)

So go your way, travel your road.
I hope your days are good.
Just remember you have kin who loves
you lots far from your own neighborhood.

August 16

Eat Carefully, Speak Carefully

Mouthfuls of anything can be very dangerous. Take pretzels for example: you have to eat pretzels one at a time to truly enjoy the flavor, the texture, the salt bits, and the way they sort of slip around your tongue. A careful, considerate consumption of pretzels is one of those enjoyable things in life, a treat that begs for a continued relationship.

However, throw a handful into the mouth, and it's a whole different story. You have difficulty breathing, you can't talk, you may dribble, have to sneeze, or need to do something else, which can be embarrassing. Most of all, because of the salt and dusty dough, you're very likely to choke. Many have suffered near death experiences because of a mouthful of dry pretzels.

The improper use of words has the same effect. Carefully chosen and deliberately spoken words can be an elixir of life to the receiver. The proper words can clarify your feelings, confirm your persuasion, and calm ruffled feelings. However, when used in haste without consideration, a poorly chosen mouthful of words can cause considerable embarrassment and sever trusted relationships. Just like the eating of pretzels, words too must be absorbed carefully. Your friendships, your working environment, and your family are dependent upon the texture of your words. A mouthful of pretzels can choke you to death, and a mouthful of words can kill a friendship or divide a family.

Eat your pretzels slowly, choose your words carefully.

April 90

Avoiding Caribbean Crunchies!

Sometimes, on the fast schooner of life, we are blown off course by the trivialities of human nature. Without the slightest warning, small gusts of indiscretions can swiftly turn into large gales of embarrassing confrontations.

The observant individual with an unassuming outlook can usually correct the sails and tack to avoid the shallow shoals of interpersonal shipwreck. However, when the barnacles of life destroy the smoothness of the hull, when rust and corrosion weaken the mast and rudder of communication, the erstwhile traveler can lose control, dash upon the coral, and flounder into a watery grave of social destruction.

Avoid those Caribbean Crunchies!

April 97

A Light on Your Camping Experience

Summer Camp's first night
was always full of fear and dread.
Although excited about tomorrow,
I feared the monster at the foot of my bed.

I found a light always most useful
during the long night in my tent.
On and off and on it shone
until the batteries were nearly spent.

So, this solace I decided to offer-
A word of hope among those souls
who also fear that boogies and bad guys
may spend the night biting your toes.

May 95

The Hike

Expect much traveling on your trail
that leads you to and fro.
No matter how you fix your rig,
there are many things to know.

The nights are dark, the way is long,
the trail is sometimes steep,
and you, as Robert Frost once said,
"have miles ... before you sleep."

Life is like a hiker's gait,
excitement at the start.
With rarely used trails and mountain streams
and dangers in the dark.

As time wears on and miles collect,
the feet begin to fade.
And before you reach your final goal,
you curse some decisions made.

Reaching the top brings new joy
and the thrill of unfettered views.
Also, the hope that hiking and life
are worth the constant abuse.

May 08

Living Beyond Ennui

God's plan for man is not to know
what things will happen tomorrow,
for wreck and ruin may be our draw
and we could not stand the sorrow.

A day at a time is all we get,
and that's not guaranteed.
Enjoy your moments; trust in Him,
for His promise is all you need.

Why know what the future holds?
Why have knowledge before it's time?
Understanding all is not our call,
not worth the worry, the whimper, the whine.

Imagine the gift we would lose
if we knew about tomorrow.
Excitement and awe would go away
when struck by life's ennui arrow.

Motivation in life is bearing strife
each day as we progress
toward a time when we won't find
anything that causes duress.

Another year has made an appearance.
Our decisions will make it matter.
A year is but a speck of time
filled with our short life's clatter.

Until that time, when we're supine
and are singing with angels on high,
we'll forget our moments of desperation
and will never see another year die.

I may not know what my future holds
while sweat on this earth I give.
But I am promised a bright, new tomorrow
When with Jesus I will eternally live

January 05

The Roads We Travel

Change the oil, check the tires, wash the car. Make a final run to a grocery store, give the neighbor the house key. Fit ten cubic feet of luggage and boxes into a five-cubic foot trunk. No, the cat cannot go with us! Be sure to turn off the stove, the TV, the iron. What do you mean the dryer is full of wet clothes!?! What did you do with my swimming trunks? Let's go, it's getting late; we want to get there before dark. Give the kids something to keep them quiet on the trip-for goodness sakes, not crayons, they melt. Okay, has everyone used the bathroom? Just a friendly warning, we're not stopping for over two hundred miles. I don't want to hear any more questions about how soon we are going to get there. No, you cannot sit in the front seat! Michelle, stop hitting Matthew, and get on your side of the car. Okay, who put the cat into the trunk. No, we're not there yet. We've only gone seven miles. Why don't we play the license plate game? Fifty points if you see one from Hawaii. No fighting in the back seat. No, we're not there yet! Matthew, get on your side of the road! I mean move to the other side of the car, NOW! I told you, we're not stopping for two hundred miles. What do you mean you didn't have to go then? You'll have to do it beside the road. I don't know if the motel has a swimming pool. We may never get to the hotel at this rate. No, we're not there yet. Matthew, do you want me to stop this car and come back there? Please, don't cry. Okay, okay, we'll stop. Who wants a coke? No, I distinctly did not say you could have a root beer float. No, we're not there yet. Michelle, why didn't you go at the last stop? Look at the cow. No, I don't know why cows have horns. What do you mean you're hungry? Yes, a hamburger would taste good.

No, we can't stop now. We haven't even crossed the state line. The state line isn't drawn with anything, son, it's an imaginary border. Yes, I'm sure they would like for you to draw a line for them. Next time we cross the line, I'll let you out so you can work on it while we go home. Hey, Nicole, look! Railroad tracks! Do you know how I can tell a train just went by? No, no, no, good try, but no, could be, but no. How can I tell? Because I can see train tracks. No, you cannot hit Daddy while he's driving. And no, we're not there yet. No, we are not stopping again. We're moving, and we want to keep moving until we get there. No, I don't know what's purple and has three rings. No, we're not there yet. We still have about two hundred miles. Let's play a game! It's called the quiet game...

May 98

A Thought as We Say Good Night

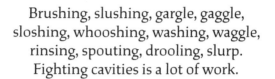

Brushing, slushing, gargle, gaggle,
sloshing, whooshing, washing, waggle,
rinsing, spouting, drooling, slurp.
Fighting cavities is a lot of work.

June 90

A Dream About Michelle

While I cannot interpret this dream, I can tell you about it.

It was a sunny day. Just you and I were riding bicycles through beautiful woods. I remember we came to a very steep bank, and we were deciding how to best get down the hill. I noticed a rocky pathway to one side and decided to try it before you did. It was a rough ride, but it was possible. I made it without any trouble.

I remember sitting at the bottom of the hill, looking up to you saying, *"The path I took works! It's a little rough, but it works, and you will safely make it down."*

You looked at my path and looked over the edge, saying you were going to come down a different way. I cried for you to follow my way, but you refused. The trail you took was straight down the bank. It looked smooth because it was muddy, and it was very steep. I again called to you, trying to get you to come down my trail. The next I knew, you started down the slippery, muddy slope. You quickly picked up speed, and before I knew it, you were airborne astraddle your bike. You were screaming as you came down. I was crying and screaming for you. Then there was this great loud kerplunk as you landed in a mud hole at the foot of the bank. I will never forget that sound or my feelings as I ran to you. The bike was still standing up in the mud. You were still sitting on the bicycle. You had a funny look on your face, but you did not say a word.

Carefully, I picked you up in my arms and started to walk away ... then I woke up.

Love Dad
July 93

A Dream About Matthew

While I cannot interpret this dream, I can tell you about it.

Seems as though you, Mom, and I were walking through some jungle somewhere in Southeast Asia. As we walked along a raging river, you stopped and listened to something.

While mom and I could not hear it, you could. Suddenly, without warning, you dived into the river and started swimming toward a still spot on the other side of the river. I became very worried for you, cried out your name, and started praying for you. You swam up to a weed-incrusted bank and pulled out a baby. Then you started to swim back across swam the river with the baby in your arms. I kept praying for you.

After you slowly walked out of the river, you set the child down and started to care for the child. As you did so, I saw a huge wave in the water. A giant serpent was swimming toward you. I frantically called out your name and told you to get away from there. You hesitated and still were talking to the child. As the giant snake came out of the water, you told the child to run away. You then turned to the snake and started walking backwards away from the creature. I kept calling out your name and yelling you to also turn and run as fast as you could. You seemed almost transfixed by the snake as you slowly backed up. The snake was getting closer and close. My heart went out for you, and I cried for you ... then I woke up.

Love Dad
July 94

Dealing with the Challenges of Being Old ...

The Move

Moved my father today.
Really didn't want to.
Almost killed me.
Who knows what it's doing to him?

Moved my father today
from his home of 40 years.
A shock to my system.
Can only imagine how he feels.

Moved my father today.
He took some furniture,
but all he really had left
were piles of memories.

Moved my father today.
He's going to a better place.
Companionship, good food
mean little at a time like this.

Moved my father today
Then walked through an empty house.
Maybe someday
it will create memories for another.

Moved my father today.
I could tell he was really sad.
His shoulders stooped
under a heavy load of tears.

July 99

Lying In My Bed In Room 12A

Peering through my bedroom window
with music of spring in the air.
Couldn't find a rhyme or reason
or anyone this moment to share.

Memories of friends, times, and youth
is all I have left to live.
Couldn't find a rhyme or reason
or anyone this moment to give.

Days feel long, time is vague,
muddles of pain sometimes swell.
Couldn't find a rhyme or reason
or anyone this moment to tell.

Was it yesterday, fifty years or more,
walking the hills and enjoying the rain.
Couldn't find a rhyme or reason
or anyone this moment to explain.

Where am I? Really couldn't say.
Feel muzzled by a mist of forgotten lore.
Couldn't find a rhyme or reason
or anyone this moment to explore.

In my stupor, shadows of light
roll over me with shades of love pure.
Couldn't find a rhyme or reason
or anyone in this moment so secure.

Feel no pain, rest comes sweet.
Spring and Angels now round me fly.
Found the rhymes, found the reason,
found the One whom I can rely.

April 04

The Wanderer

The old man shuffles along
with a mind that is askew,
hardly a moment passes
without looking at something that's new.

He lives his life in foggy frustration.
Can't grasp his reason to live.
He takes much love and perspiration
and in return has little to give.

A willow smile and forgetful phrases
is all he can accomplish.
Moments of bliss forever stay
in the soul of his misty mantras.

He took my hand. He trusted me.
With a demure that's gawky and slow,
he looks for something he'll never see
that happened a lifetime ago.

With quizzing eyes and listing gait,
he wonders his shortening paths.
A world of unknown life awaits
as thick as the darkest morass.

Should he define his whole existence
with only a stumble and stare?
Or can this man who no one listens
build in us a legacy of care?

Dedicated to Lloyd, my forever friend
August 05

Sweet as a Plum

As sweet as a plum, this little Mom
can win hearts with only a glance.
Who knows her mind or sees her soul,
Who? But those who give her a chance.

With honest delight, a heartfelt sight,
this lady before faded youth.
A lifetime ago before the snow,
and the unimagined became her truth.

The mystic friends she meets each day
stir images she cannot command.
Now her reflection is slipping away
like grains of wind sifted sand.

Memories of life that once were dear
are forever locked in a murky mist.
All she has no more counts
as she edges toward her final abyss.

Remembering Bette ...
August 02

Caught Red Handed

Honoring Long-Term Caregivers ...

Do unto others is a God given creed.
Without others knowing are you indeed?
A miracle? An angel? To those with a need.

To bring others joy without them knowing
is a mission above all for which you are showing
the true spirit of kindness and a love overflowing.

Without fanfare, without a hope of cheers,
you have silently helped a soul remove some tears.
A source for strength that can linger for years.

You expected no gratitude whatsoever.
But you were seen in your private endeavor.
This token in your honor is to keep forever.

Although small and not very splendid,
remember with grace, for you are being
commended.
After all, you were caught doing good Red Handed.

Especially Alisha ...
November 09

Welcome to the Million Mile Club

*To all those wonderful Long-Term
Care Angels I have known*

Because of you,
many lives have brightened,
many needs were met,
much love was offered,
and lest we forget
the extra miles you've gone,
that extra smile you gave,
that long walk down the hallway,
that extra time you prayed.
Do what you do.
Do it with pride.
Very few can.
You're a million-mile person,
without a marching band.

May 2010

The Death of My Father

———————•———————

Quietness stifles. The room is heavy.
Hushed breathing roars in the ear.
We are praying. Father is dying.
I believe he's anxious to go somewhere.

A restless figure on a bed of pure white,
unable to speak, eyes closed tight.
Lips now dry, once were alive
with laughter and talk, now not a sigh.

A throaty rasp, a tear of sadness,
a cough for breath. One facing the end
forever to forget heartache and sorrow.
This life he's leaving, a new one begins.

A quiet gasp, sullen silence.
A dreaded fear fills the air.
A peaceful moment, a lingering hope,
then we feel eternity is near.

The Spirit consoles, the moment has come.
Hearts left are heavy, comfort remains.
Though a glass darkly, a victory was won.
Dad finds peace in the arms of the Son.

February 14, 2007

Graveside Reminiscences

Sitting on a hillside chair,
overlooking a valley fair,
a flag draped casket looms in sight.
Dad is gone.

Thinking about this lovely place,
realizing Dad would soon embrace
the stone-cold ground of Maple Hill.
Dad is gone.

Waves of sadness swell inside.
Grasp a hand in which to hide
memories that dwell within.
Dad is gone.

Cousins abound gather around,
Uncles gone into the ground.
Only us left, the next generation.
Dad is gone.

Taps are played, large tears parade.
A veteran's salute, then Dad is laid ...
Sitting on a hillside chair,
overlooking a valley fair.
Dad is gone.

February 2007

The Death of My Stepmother

My daughter, Michelle, has a unique sense of humor and a unique perspective on nearly everything. Just before I left my hometown of Pulaski, Virginia after burying my stepmother, she called and tried to console me. She came up with a beautiful image: *"Dad"* she said, *"About now, grand-mom is going through orientation."*

Jesus and the angels are probably, at this moment, taking her around Heaven, showing her the ropes, telling her how things are done, what to expect, introducing her to neighbors on the street where her mansion has been prepared, and telling her about the upcoming great supper of the Lamb.

I'll bet also at this very moment, Grand-mom is taking a break from the tour to have lunch with her sisters, Gin, Cecil, and Margaret, and her mother, Sally, where they could be talking about old times and talking about what they will be doing for the rest of eternity.

Michelle went on to say that my stepmother could even be meeting my birthmother, Ruth, who was telling her *"Thank you"* for taking over and raising her children.

Now, I'm not sure of the biblical credibility of Michelle's imaginary. However, her message is soothing and points to the hope of all of us Christians. Mom is enjoying herself; she is in utter peace; she has no physical afflictions now. She is being bathed in the love of Jesus.

Soon, I, Debbie my sister, Valerie my wife, my other children, and, most assuredly, Michelle will all be together with my mother, my stepmother, and my dad, enjoying Heaven!

February 2004

I'm There

You say you never see me.
I'll forever believe you do.
You'll see me every moment
as I keep seeing you.

A crowded room, a lonely walk,
with every thought you'll find.
Even though no hand you hold,
you'll see me in your mind.

A gentle touch, a wistful voice
of someone we'll never forget.
Stirring thoughts of moon lit walks
with a mystery we barely met.

Melancholy are some moments
as you reminisce of days gone by.
You say you never see me.
I'm that tear in the corner of your eye.

December 1999

The most personal of all my writings …

Explain the Miss

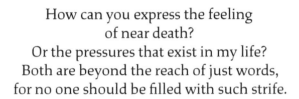

How can you express the feeling
of near death?
Or the pressures that exist in my life?
Both are beyond the reach of just words,
for no one should be filled with such strife.

I cannot explain the guilt and the blame
that overshadows my thoughts when I think
or feel the pain when I try to rename
the cause for my terrible life shrink.

The body is torn, the mind is forlorn.
Emotions are merely a sham.
Only one level of thought fills my mind:
why am I here, and what became of this man?

Pressures abound that continually surround
my life and all that I love.
Holding the course with constant remorse
couldn't be done without help from above

If I seem down, that would be good.
For down is better than I am.
I'm below the worst with deep silent hurts
with barely a glimmer of hope to my plans.

What does it mean when all of my dreams
that once were, are nearly extinct?
Why is it when we try to finally satisfy,
the worst is all we can expect?

If it goes wrong, it will with no doubt.
A given, no matter how hard we try.
When hopes are dashed, when dreams are crashed,
our best emotion is only to cry.

A struggle with debt is all we get
when we try to figure a way
to climb over the wall and get on the ball
and clean up the debts we must pay.

I know it is wrong to feel so forlorn,
but feeling this way is a must.
When in a great trial with no view of a sail,
there is only one on whom we must trust.

In all of our pleadings, and in all of our kneeing's,
our prayers are constant and true
because of this thing, our hearts must soon sing
when that rainbow finally breaks through.

May 2005

The Cold of November

Wish I could write a poem
that would cause me to remember
the good time of my life
before the cold of November.

When I was a pup, it was so good to live.
When things were up, enough money to give.
A future ahead with excitement abound.
Walking on air, I'm now on the ground.

Dreams are dimmer. Where is the hope?
Wanting to give with only energy to mope.
Not fair, I cry, too soon to just die.
Not the grave, far worse.
My dreams say goodbye.

Will it all end? These times of travail.
Or must I go on and keep hanging my tail?
I'd change my life. I already have.
A different person I am, gone a little mad.

I'll not blame God. It's my sins, I see,
that brought me down to this desperate plea.
My coming of age brings
inspection with strife.
A shifting toward more tension in life.

I once had high hopes. I looked far beyond.
Now all I see is a life that's forlorn ...
Help! Is my call. From my miry life dis.
Surely, I'll fall into some new life of bliss.

What is the answer? If only I knew.
I'm living on faith, this I know to be true.
Is my life designed to crash and maim?
Or can I find a new target to aim?

Mercy! I cry, *God relieve my pain!*
Bring me up to a much higher plain.
Meanwhile, I'll remember
life before the Cold of November.

November 2004

Foolish Decisions

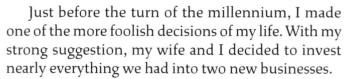

Just before the turn of the millennium, I made one of the more foolish decisions of my life. With my strong suggestion, my wife and I decided to invest nearly everything we had into two new businesses.

With what she and I thought were enough prayers and discussions, we decided to make the move. We did not know it was a decision that would change our lives forever.

When you read this, you will know the final results of our leap of faith. As this is being written, we have no idea how this will work itself out or what will happen in the meantime. Believe me, right now, I wish I could see this from your perspective. Because in your hands is the complete story, all the way to the end. On my side of the pencil there is a great unknown, a dread of much work to do, many decisions to be made, a reliance on many good people whom I don't know well, and a seemingly impossible situation to overcome. As you read this, you will know just how strong my faith in God is. You will know just how much work it took to successfully make the impossible work. You're reading what I'm now living.

I'm writing this for more than one reason. First, writing about my daily battles with finances, payables, government agencies, staffing, dealings with people, personal dread, and my overwhelming depression is a catharsis. Also, when I write this down, I must think about what is going on. When I see it on paper, I seem to be better able to meet the demands of the moment and to plan for my next move.

Beginning at the Beginning

Early in 1999, an acquaintance approached me about purchasing her boarding homes. Because I have been involved in the industry in various dimensions, including an owner for ten years, I took a serious interest in her proposal. Another acquaintance was very unhappy about his situation at the time. He felt his talents were not being used to their fullest extent. Because he was a close personal friend, I knew about his feelings. When I was approached, I, in turn, approached my friend. We talked and decided to really look into the situation. He had no funds, but I had some equity in one of my businesses. In our discussions, we determined that if I could come up with the money, he would move to Vancouver and manage the businesses. Again, with much prayer, soul searching, and figuring on paper, we decided we could do it.

The Following Is Scary, True, and Encouraging

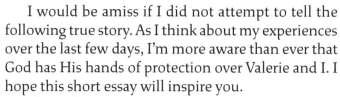

I would be amiss if I did not attempt to tell the following true story. As I think about my experiences over the last few days, I'm more aware than ever that God has His hands of protection over Valerie and I. I hope this short essay will inspire you.

About three weeks ago, while in my office doing paperwork and trying to figure out how we were going to pay the Rose Ranch bills, the intercom rang. *"Dan, you have visitors in the lobby. They look official."* Val was outside, saw the people come in, and thought the state boarding home license inspectors were paying us a visit. Knowing it was time for our annual inspection, I was not too worried as I approached the lady and gentleman. Then they showed me their badges and said they were from the IRS. Needless to say, I was somewhat taken aback. I invited them to my office to find out what they wanted.

Now, I already knew we had owed the government one month of 941 (payroll taxes) for Columbia Place, a business we sold in 2004. I had already talked to whoever you talk to when you call the IRS 800 number. At that time, the person at the other end did not know how much we owed and said they would contact the local field office who would in turn contact me. That was seven months earlier in December of 2004. I figured I would get a letter or at least a phone call telling me how much I owed. I also figured that if we didn't have enough money, I would try to set up a payment plan. I knew we did not owe much more than $6,000. I placed this information in the back of my mind and went about my business, almost, but not quite, forgetting about this obligation-at least until that eventful morning. I still remember the agents asking for information and documents from years past. I knew somewhere in our files we had what they wanted, but because I was so nervous, I was unable to find much of what they needed. Although I had no cause to be, I must have looked suspicious.

During our discussion, they told us we owed $15,000. I nearly fell out of my chair! Most of what we owed turned out to be fines and interest. I told them Columbia Place no longer existed and we had no money, the only thing left in the Columbia Place checking account was $100. They asked me to write a check for that amount. After a couple of hours, we set up a second meeting for the following Monday where I would present the additional information they needed. Because we did not have that much cash, my only hope was to set up some type of payment plan even though I did not know how we were going to pay. Cash flow at Rose Ranch was not all that great.

After they left, I called my accountant. At this same time, he was finishing up the 2004 Tax report for Columbia Place and Rose Ranch. "Dan," he said, "do you realize you have over $350,000 in capital gains from selling Columbia Place?"

In my feeble defense, Columbia Place was the first business I had ever sold. Capital gains is that "hidden" tax that any good businessman would know about and be able to deal with, BEFORE they sold their business! This bit of news was completely out of left field for this novice entrepreneurial care provider. I then entered his figures into my Turbo Tax program, and I realized I owed nearly $60,000 in income taxes.

Again, all of this happened the same day.

I didn't have money to pay the $15,000, much less this! Now, just to let you know where I'm coming from, Val and I feel we are in a ministry as we provide a service to those individuals who are aged, handicapped, and in some cases, have dementia. Val once said as we were moving to Vancouver to run Rose Ranch that it felt like we were going to a mission's field without any sponsorship. We really do feel what we are doing is unique. But this morning, I wondered if I had taken us down the wrong road that was leading to financial oblivion. How could all of this be happening if we were doing God's will?

In a flash, I was crying out in my spirit. *"Lord, we need Your help. The world is crashing down around us. Please, help!"*

Talk about utter despair. I was feeling it that day. I was absolutely floored; at the bottom of my normally optimistic reserves, I was devastated, depressed, and disillusioned. In fact, it felt as if I were drowning and gasping for breath. My head was spinning. I had absolutely no hope in sight. I wondered what the IRS could do to me. I had heard stories. Would they take away everything? No words can describe how I was feeling. I went home, grabbed my Bible, and went to my private study. I cried out, *"Lord, I'm at the end. I'm trying so hard, I'm tired, and I'm failing. This day is so overwhelmingly unbelievable. I must have Your help!"* Although I can't remember ever doing this in my life, I laid the Bible down and said, *"Lord, You must help. I'm just going to open my Bible, and I pray You will show me what I need."* Now, I would never recommend anyone do this, but at that moment, I was totally lost. This was my only hope.

The Bible fell open to Psalm 69. *"Save me, O God for the waters have come up to my neck. I sink in the miry depths where there is no foothold. I have come into the deep waters; the floods engulf me."*

Wow, look at those words. This Bible passage was describing me at that very moment. He was talking to me. I wrote in the margin: "July 8, 2005, this is me today."

"I am worn out calling for help, my throat is parched. My eyes fail, looking for my God."

At this moment, I realized that God really was talking to me. Relief began to build as I remembered He *does* love me. He *does* care for me. As I read these first few passages, I had an immediate assurance that this experience in my life would be overcome.

Reading on: *"I am forced to restore what I did not steal."* Boy, did that ring a bell. Then He struck home. *"You know my folly, O God; my guilt is not hidden from you."* I was reminded that God knew my every thought, and that my sins, both secret and public, were known by Him. I also realized that He knew my desire was to serve Him foremost in my life. Nothing was hidden from Him.

"Oh, Lord," I cried, *"forgive me for my weakness."*

Then came another forceful portion of this scripture: *"May those who hope in you not be disgraced because of me ..."*

Please, I thought.

"O Lord, the Lord Almighty; may those who seek you not be put to shame because of me."

I prayed that no matter what happened to me because of what was happening, I would not jeopardize the soul of anyone who looked upon me as being God's servant. Then I read on, and the thirteenth verse said, "But I pray to you, O Lord, in the time of your favor; in your great love, O God, answer me with your sure salvation."

It came to me. The answer was for me to continue praying until God fulfilled His purpose. No matter what was going on around me, my only hope was to trust in Him. My heart began to sing, and I again had a spiritual lift in my step. I knew-I just knew- that things would work out. God was going to perform a miracle.

Then, one final verse stood out. Verse seventeen says, "Do not hide your face from your servant; answer me quickly, for I am in trouble."

Two days later, I received a call from the IRS. "Dan, because the company [Columbia Place] is no more, we know there is no way we can collect the penalties and interest. However, you must pay the 941 trust funds. That is your employees' money. When can you give us a check for $4800?"

The next morning, I took them the check. At the same time, I was working with my accountant. "Is there anything that is legal that can be done to reduce the capital gains tax?"

"I'll get back to you," he said. A few days later, he called. "There are a few additional deductions that we can do, and I did discover something important. You have a loss that I did not consider, and it amounts to $147,000. Now re-figure your taxes."

I did, and instead of owing $60,000, I "only" owed $5,000. Now, neither the $4,800 nor the $5,000 is walking around money, but the possible $75,000 is knock me to the floor money. No way could I pay that. God heard my cry, used His Word to encourage me, and allowed a financial miracle to happen. Now, all I have to do is thank Him.

This story is a result of my promise. And there's more. (Seriously.)

December 2002 was the toughest, most remarkable, scariest, stressful, most unique December of my life. December 2002 was really a month of fire, flood, wind, despair, and financial drought. I discovered true moments of desperate hopelessness.

Nothing went right in December. Yet in the end, everything went right. Nothing went smooth in December, yet in the end, everything worked. Everything was broken in December, yet in the end, everything worked. It was a month of make it or break it. Valerie and I had actually reached the wall. We had absolutely nowhere else to go. We prayed constantly. Dreadful thoughts filled our mind.

I entered the month extremely worried because there was no way we could have Christmas for our family. There was no way we could pay our personal bills, our company's bills, much less salaries for Rose Ranch, Columbia Place and The Seasons employees.

We had reached bottom.

All of our properties had a financial shortfall. Rose Ranch was the worst. The census at Rose Ranch was down. One of our residents passed away, another went to the hospital, a third went to a nursing home, and another (a private resident) fell and broke her leg.

Another resident even had a stroke and went to the hospital. Our cash flow had collapsed. Despair filled my heart. I really could do nothing but pray. *Because* of the last three years, I learned to pray. God placed us in a trial period of our life, and we had hit bottom.

Early in the month, as the residents were having their evening meal, we had some

excitement. We looked out of the dining room window and saw sparks and bright flashes of light on the roof of our annex building. There was a major short somewhere in the building, and the power lines leading into the building were literally melting.

The fire department came, the PUD came, and the fire alarm company came. We figured out the cause was a burned-out electric furnace that had *really* burned out. Thank goodness for our friend Vern- God's Tin Man (Furnace Installer). We were able to repair it at a reasonable cost.

For the last week of December, Valerie and I were completely stressed out. We had reached our end. The pressure of getting or not getting a much-needed refinancing loan was becoming too great for either of us to withstand. There was a spirit of heaviness over both of us. I felt we were again standing in front of a large black wall with no way to go through it. We needed a miracle. We needed relief. We needed God to help us.

I was told that at the closing of the refinancing, we would have to have between twelve and eighteen thousand dollars available to pay off final obligations such as delinquent taxes, the final month's interest, additional loans, and other closing costs. We were worried. I did not have any money, much less the needed $18,000. I began the proceedings to cash out an IRA for some of the money. Matthew, my son, also said he could raise a little, and I was willing to apply some of it to a credit card. But that still would not be enough. We had completely run out of our financial resources. Two weeks before everything was supposed to come to a head. My friend, Chaplain Roger Wolfe, gave a message under the anointing of the Holy Spirit to the Congregation of our church. As I was listening, he said not to worry about your homes, jobs, or corporations. When he said "corporations", my heart leaped. Why did he say corporations? Was that message meant for Val and me?

The Sunday before the scheduled Monday signing date, I went forward during prayer time and asked Roger to pray for me. I then started to pray, and he just listened. When I had finished, he said to me, *"Don't worry, everything is in God's hands, He is in control of this situation. You will accomplish His will in this situation. You will bring God's love to the people with whom you work. God's timing is perfect."*

The next day, the day when we were supposed to sign, the Title Company called and said there were some problems and we would not be able to sign on this day, but hopefully tomorrow. Tomorrow was the 31st of December. From what I understood, we had to close and get the money by the 31st or the deal was off.

On the morning of the 31st, we were told to be at the Title Company to sign papers at 11:00. We still had not been told how much money was needed. The last word was between twelve and eighteen thousand dollars. I had blank checks but no money in the bank. I had the crazy idea that they would allow me to postdate a check until the funds from my IRA arrived. I still had nothing in the bank. We were stressed to say the least.

About halfway to the office where we were supposed to sign, I realized I had not brought along ANY checks, good or bad. Because of the time, I could not go back and get any. I just prayed. The tension was building. We were showed into a room where the signing would happen. Val and I prayed that God would take charge of the proceedings and make it a smooth event and give us the wisdom to deal with whatever came up. We started signing papers. I was wondering when I would need to produce the $18,000.

Halfway through the signing, our banker lady got a phone call from the head person in San Francisco. Hold it a moment, there was trouble in our back ground check. They had missed a lean that a food company had against our business. I talked to the lady. I explained the situation and that I had paid off the food company. The information they had found was wrong. I was told to produce documentation that proved my statement. I told them I would and the signing continued. I was still worried about the $18,000. As we neared completion of the signing, we were presented with a paper that stated how all of the finances were to be distributed. I looked at the bottom line and saw $23,000.

My heart almost stopped. Oh no! I could never get that much money. I asked the lady if everything was correct on the form. "*Why, yes.*"

I looked at the bottom line again. "*Err, this $23,000, is this what I have to pay today?*"

She looked at the form. "*No, no, you don't have to pay that. That is the amount of the surplus funds. You will be getting a check for that amount.*"

As our bank officer looked at the form, she immediately called her office in San Francisco. "*Is this correct?*" I heard her say. "*Can they get this money now? They can!*"

My heart was now leaping. I was in a state of shock. The tension refused to leave, yet I sensed something was happening. Not wanting to rock the ship anymore, I quietly said, "*Are we through?*"

"*Yes.*"

"*You mean I don't have to sign anything else?*"

"*No.*"

"*You mean, I don't need any money now?*"

"*No.*"

"*You mean, we can leave?*"

"*Yes, we are finished.*"

My soul was shouting. My heart was leaping. My mind was in a daze. Quietly, we left. I shouted under my breath. "*Valerie, do you realize what just happened?* **God is good***!*"

January 2002

Daniel L. French | 57

Good, all of that is over now, I feel much better.

He Has Given Everything.

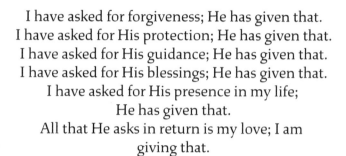

I have asked for forgiveness; He has given that.
I have asked for His protection; He has given that.
I have asked for His guidance; He has given that.
I have asked for His blessings; He has given that.
I have asked for His presence in my life;
He has given that.
All that He asks in return is my love; I am
giving that.

He asks that I remember Him in time of trouble;
I will do that.
He asks that I put Him first; I will do that.
He asks that I acknowledge His blessings;
I will do that.
He asks that I have faith in Him; I will do that.
He asks that I wait upon Him; I will do that.
What *I* ask is for me, what *He* asks for is a better me.

12/15/2004

My Backyard …

Little birds, cute to watch,
flutter from limb to limb.
Pecking the ground, flapping around,
light as a feather on the wind.

Eyeing the cat, high up they sat,
waiting for the moment so sweet.
When all is clear, then dinner is near
and hungry beaks break up the suet.

Seeds and nuts, food filled trays,
waiting for their short brisk scramble.
With seeds a flying, these birds are trying
to gobble up more than seems ample.

A Longing for the Sun ...

Ridgefield Sunshine (or the lack thereof)

A rare delight a moment of bright.

Only a moment; nevermore.

A surprise that seems a jest.

Lifting souls, letting go.

Ahhh, Oooh, where'd it go?

Good night! Whatta light! ...Goodbye.

My Garden Mysteries

Could it be, the old shade tree
holds mysteries I'll never know.

Could I spot my flowered lot
with secrets all fully composed.

Could the birds, without any words,
know more than I suspect.

Maybe I'm goofy, or a little spoofy
when wondering my garden's bequest.

Can it happen when I'm napping,
when that moment of Magic flows.

When fruits go crazy, flowers not lazy,
and the vegetables appear in neat rows.

When rhubarb is sweet, and sweet peas secrete
a fragrance that tickles the nose.

When beans and corn and pumpkins grow,
and the beets and broccoli I cultivate.

When buds come out, and when they sprout,
why can't I see the ovulate?

Where am I, and why don't I spy
when mysteries my garden advances.

When it gives yield and brings me joys
when my seeds become posies and pansies!

July 2012

Two Doves Once Flew into My Yard

Two doves once flew into my yard.
A turtle dove and it's mate.
They came at dawn and again at eve.
Spending good times at my bird food plate.

You could tell the one loved the other.
A gentleman squire was he.
He watched the sky for friend or foe
while his loved one ate happily.

To watch them frisk around the yard
with nary a care on their mind.
Their banter was light, their teasing was bright,
and their moments seemed so sublime.

I could tell there was love
as they sat far above somewhere in a tree.
The cooing of the male I'm sure is sweet
to the ear of the mate-to-be.

A lifelong love, planned from above.
A no cuter feather than she.
Given a choice, no sweeter a chorus
then cooing designed for his sweet.

One day, the sun did not shine.
Then only one dove I saw.
With a slowing gait and a silent ache,
he lost his best friend of all.

We're not promised a thing tomorrow.
Life is quick, for bird or man.
No sheltering house, nor sharing spouse,
so, enjoy the cooing while you can.

November 2013

Enjoy the Moment

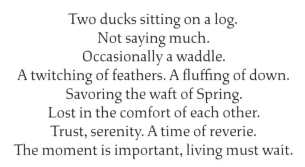

Two ducks sitting on a log.
Not saying much.
Occasionally a waddle.
A twitching of feathers. A fluffing of down.
Savoring the waft of Spring.
Lost in the comfort of each other.
Trust, serenity. A time of reverie.
The moment is important, living must wait.

March 2009

I Met Fred

I had a visitor today.
Fred the Squirrel came to play.
He found a friendly place to be,
but didn't have time to play with me.

Walked the fence, climbed a tree,
ran around, chased a bee,
fluttered his tail, wiggled his nose,
stopped in stride; checking, I suppose.

The birds that flew over his head,
the cat that surely was his dread
walked a wire way up high,
balanced by tail and maybe the sky

Never thought he'd come to me,
although his friend I'd like to be.
Imagine talking to a squirrel.
The stories, the tales, about his world.

Enjoy yourself, make a furrow.
Enjoy the seeds left out for sparrow.
Fill your jowls, work your cheeks,
store in nest for winter's weeks.

August 2016

A Genuine Old-Fashioned House Plant Kit

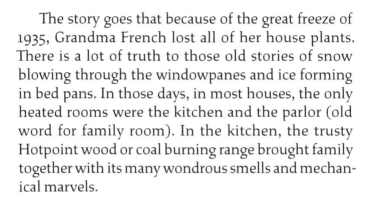

The story goes that because of the great freeze of 1935, Grandma French lost all of her house plants. There is a lot of truth to those old stories of snow blowing through the windowpanes and ice forming in bed pans. In those days, in most houses, the only heated rooms were the kitchen and the parlor (old word for family room). In the kitchen, the trusty Hotpoint wood or coal burning range brought family together with its many wondrous smells and mechanical marvels.

Grandma French's new Youngstown stove featured a warming shelf above the range top (where uneaten biscuits and country ham waited for a mid-morning snack), a built-in water tank that heated water for dishes, washing and bathing; and the most mysterious, incredible and dangerous gadget of all, a clean out trap on the stove pipe that occasionally blackened the unlucky person in charge of cleaning soot from the chimney, or the unlucky kid that bumped it while playing kitchen tag. But this story digresses.

Because of the great freeze of 1935, Grandma French lost most of her house plants. Yearning for a little greenery in the old homestead, she took a few old canning jars from a shelf in the smokehouse and a few old sweet potatoes from the root cellar. Only a few lucky persons have seen and smelled a genuine root cellar like Grandma's. It was dark, dank, cool and full of mystery. Kids and cousins would dare each other to go into its recesses and close the hatch. Only the really brave ones would venture into that totally dark space amidst the many bushels of apples, potatoes, onions, carrots, possible mice, spiders, garter snakes and a most unique smell that only can be described as, *smelling like the taste of sprouts people nowadays eat on their sandwiches*. But again, I digress.

Because of the great freeze of 1935, Grandma French lost most of her house plants. To help her overcome her dearth of green finery, she took some sweet potatoes from the cellar, old unusable mason canning jars from the smoke house, and a little water from the back-porch water rain barrel. With these items, and with little trouble, Grandma could turn the house into a green oasis at any time throughout the year. Grandma used water from the rain barrel off the back porch because she didn't want to use water from the springhouse.

The springhouse was almost a half mile away from the main house, the walk back to the farmhouse was uphill, over rocky ground, around a chicken coup, and through the potato patch–and two-gallon buckets of water are heavy. To have drinking and cooking water, someone had to carry them from the springhouse to the kitchen every morning and every evening. For whatever reason, the smallest kid in the family usually got this job (and he better not "*muddy the water*"). One more thing; the water needed could not be carried in one trip. Grandma didn't get indoor plumbing until 1951 and an indoor toilet until 1957. But I digress.

Because of the great freeze of 1935, grandma French lost most of her house plants. She knew how to solve her problems with little fuss, and so could you with a small amount of cool rainwater, an old mason jar, and a sweet potato about ready to seed. Own your own authentic, old-fashioned house plant and step back into the youth of Grandma French. A time when things were simpler, people were friend-lier, church was the major community social center, you didn't mind walking four miles through three feet of snow to a one room school, you knew your neighbor, weed was something you hoed, pot was something in which you cooked taters, greens, and groundhog, and a $50 houseplant could not be found. But I digress.

October 1986

The Cold of Virginia

Gnarly trees, cold stiff breeze,
scenes of a gray, bitter bright day.
Blue Ridge hills, old saw mills.
Winter time in Virginia.

Grass looks dead, dirt looks red.
People about, brave to go out.
Old dog howls, houses with boughs.
Winter time in Virginia.

Even with the gray sullen days,
hope of spring never fades.
The darkest of time can always promise
Springtime in Virginia.

Sitting in a plane in Roanoke Virginia
February 2007

Our home in Lacey, Washington was for sale,
This letter to potential purchasers was instrumental in the
house selling quickly.

Welcome to the French Home.

We have lived in this house for thirteen years. It has become a part of us. However, obligations and circumstances are now forcing us to sell and move on.

I wrote this note because I wanted you to know a little about our home and how we feel about it. First, the building is not perfect. We know that. However, there could be a no more perfect home. Our three kids went through their teenage years in this house. We went through auto accidents, school concerts, football games, band trips, church outings, and many prayerful moments in this house. It is filled with more than our furniture; it is filled with memories. God has blessed this home with great neighbors, beautiful scenery, a great place to walk, a private lakeside park, and a sense of security. I'm glad to say we will leave the new owner a clean slate where their family memories can be created.

Five or six years ago, we added the back room to the house; we call it our "great room." We spend most of our time in this room. The "great room" has seen many parties, friends, overnighters, TV movies, and, of course, food. My wife likes French doors, so I made sure she got her wish. By the way, the outside doors are made by Anderson; the best. Just like my wife. She had been asking for hardwood floors for years. I told her when the kids left home and the dog died, we'd get them. Well, the dog died. A few years ago, we came back from an October business trip back east. The first rain of the year leaked through the roof on the eastside of the dining room. The insurance paid to have the roof repaired and the carpet replaced. I decided to kick in a few extra bucks and put in her hardwood floor.

We became one bedroom short as the kids grew older. I built a room in the garage for my son. He loved the privacy and the ability to sneak out at night. About the only thing left of that room is the window I had to put in, the sheet rock over part of the ceiling, and the glue marks on the floor. That space is a full time two car garage again. (Once we get all of that stuff outta there).

The upstairs office was our daughter's room. When she moved away, I spent a weekend converting her blue bedroom into the office you now see. She came back and realized that nothing would ever again be the same. Time moves on.

There are many unfinished projects around the house. We wanted to put another gas stove in the front room. My wife wanted to enlarge the mud/laundry room. At one time, we were thinking of a jacuzzi on the deck, but alas, those things will be up to the new owner.

If you should decide that this is the house for you, then our prayer is that the love our family has enjoyed in our home will overflow to your family and you will feel the same joy as you turn this house into your home.

In the front yard on the right side of the house is a pink dogwood. This is a very special tree because the ashes of Muffy, our Australian Shepherd, were placed there when we planted the tree. When we look at that tree, we think of our big-hearted, loyal pet. Someday, you will see a car drive by slowly. We will be in it, looking at what happened to the house and the "Muffy Tree."

December 2001

Front Porch Perception

Doing what almost everyone in Pulaski, Virginia does best on a warm summer evening, I find myself sitting on my family's front porch with my wife and my father. They are reading while I listen to insects chirp and songbirds sing.

As I enjoy the moment, my mind goes back to a time when our family would spend hours sitting on this porch, talking to neighbors, sipping iced tea, and trying to figure out what we would be having for supper the following evening.

The house at 220 Lake Street is like many small country homes in any small country town. Built nearly 100 years ago, the large two-story home has a front porch that stretches from one side of the house to the other. On the porch sits a glider, two rocking chairs, a small table, and numerous folding lawn chairs, just waiting for unexpected guests who could "*sit and stay awhile.*" The 220 Lake Street porch is very comfortable. Because the house faces east, a person sitting on the porch can enjoy the warm morning sun, cooling breezes even on the hottest summer afternoon, and warm summer nights, watching the twinkling of fireflies and hearing the chorus of millions of unseen insects. Sitting there in my solitude, ghosts of my past are awakened. Out of the corner of my eye, I think I see Aunt Cecil sitting in her swing at the house next door, telling me to sneak over for a piece of fried chicken. I know that at any moment,

Uncle Everett could be coming around the corner of the house with another story and a hand full of concord grapes. Across the street, Frank Millirons sits on his porch glider contentedly smoking a pipe.

Up the street, Johnny White comes out of his house with his dog close behind. Since it's a nice day, he and I play catch for a couple of hours as we prepare for the "big" game Thursday morning at Calfee Park. We tell each other stories about how great we will someday be. We talk about our sports heroes: Johnny Bench, Yogi Barra, the Mick, Don Drysdale, Whitey Ford, and a myriad of others. We really begin to "loosen up" and start "burning the ball in."

We have to step out of the street as Jake Kegley drives up and pulls into his driveway next door. His big, shiny, green 1948 Buick, roars like a big 1948 Buick. He is hungry and ready for supper after spending another day in Bland, or Wythe, or Giles County, working for the Appalachian Electric Power Company. A big friendly man, Jake's laugh can be heard throughout the neighborhood.

Also, in the quiet summer air, you can hear the unforgettable laugh of Mary Ellen Umbarger as she says goodbye to another patient. Somewhat of a local celebrity, she is the first female Chiropractor in Virginia.

As I look out over the porch banister I can see much of the south side of the Town of Pulaski. I never realized what great view property our front porch is. From the heights of Draper Mountain and Peak's Knob on the south, to the hill where Pulaski High School stands to the north is a true panoramic view that would cause land values to grow by thousands of dollars in a more sophisticated area.

In the humid, sweet, evening air, I can see the lights of Calfee Park. Tonight, the Pulaski Cubs are playing some other Appalachian D league baseball team. Suddenly, the old county courthouse clock chimes the hour. Both day and night, its bell sounds out a warm and friendly dong-dong-dong that reminds everyone within miles of the march of time. The wafting hiss of steam escaping from huge boilers at the Jefferson Mills textile plant just down the hill toggles memories of long ago, as does the far away whistle of a Norfolk and Western locomotive. In the distance there is a barking of dogs that gets louder and louder as a wave of woofs starts on one side of town and slowly moves to the other.

As I sit here thinking, I now understand I was too young to appreciate the views, the sounds, and the smells of Pulaski. Too busy thinking about baseball and girls, and too concentrated on getting through school. My youthful life in Pulaski mainly consisted of dreaming about getting out.

I did-now some forty years later.

As much as I want to, I realize I could never get back.

Much to my surprise, I did come back.

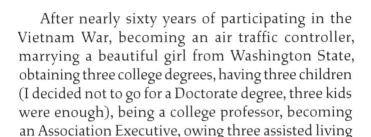

After nearly sixty years of participating in the Vietnam War, becoming an air traffic controller, marrying a beautiful girl from Washington State, obtaining three college degrees, having three children (I decided not to go for a Doctorate degree, three kids were enough), being a college professor, becoming an Association Executive, owing three assisted living facilities, and retiring in a small town in Washington State, I figured the remainder of my very exciting life was set. *"Little do we know what our future holds!"*

Be aware, this is the moment I begin my amateurish effort to transition my life story from one phase to another.

From one beautiful and God graced portion of my life, to a second example of God's mercies, unmerited favor, and direction.

As you well know, life does not go as we plan or even close to the realm of our imagination. Mine changed, and it changed quickly and drastically.

As I said, I was planning on spending the rest of my life in Washington, eating clams and shipwreck stew and playing with my grandchildren.

But God had another plan in mind.

Valerie and I had been happily married nearly fifty-one years. Then in a moment- actually, from September to January-everything changed. She discovered she had cancer, and in a sad moment in January 2019, she went to be with the Lord. I lost my wife.

Yes, for a long time after that, I was in the pits. My entire outlook on life changed. I was lost without my helpmate, my soulmate. I really lost interest in what was going on around me. I didn't care about worldly goods, worldly wealth, or doing worldly things. I knew I lost Val; I also knew I would see her again. Someday. That was my one great hope.

This was a really dark time for my family and I.

But through it all, God had other plans. He still has a purpose for my life. (Oh yes, and yours too!)

As this time in my life progressed, I fully began to remember that I was God's child, and no matter what happened to me, I was in God's hands. I loved Him, and He loved me. I continually ask for His direction, and at this time in my life, I really needed His touch.

Through a strange set of circumstances, I begin to feel God working in my life. There was no blaming God for taking Valerie away. Instead, in my heart, there was a soft assurance He was in control of everything that was happening to me. I was devastated by the loss of Valerie. At the same time, I knew in my heart I would see her again, soon.

I was sad, yet not without hope. Jesus's promise lived in my heart,

A few weeks after Valerie went to Heaven, I received an e-mail from an old friend I grew up with, sending me sympathies for my loss. It had been many years since I had seen her, and the condolences were from a friend who had also lost her spouse. Because of her loss and my loss, we were able to communicate on the same level of pain and understanding.

Over a few months, our communication grew. It grew to the point that I wanted to personally see her again.

In June of that same year, I went to Virginia for a visit.

From the start, we had a kinship. We were from the same country town, we went to the same church, knew each other from youth group, and from the sixth grade, we went to school together and graduated high school in the same class. We both suffered the same pain. We were good friends ... but never dated. I don't know the reason for that.

She went to Bible School; I went into the Air Force. We saw each other only a few times during the next fifty or so years.

Ok, now you can go on and continue to read this book because Bonnie and our new life together has beun.

Now, I must deal with a tragic event, the most terrible time of my life.

Losing My Wife

Valerie

You've been my valentine for 50 years.
Through thick and thin, laughter and tears,
We've traveled far in our glorious epic.
We've seen riches, strife, and moments hectic.

And now, looking back, I can only say,
our love has strengthened each passing day.
As the years fly by, and with hope in our King,
Our motto, of course, "enjoy simple things."

Now you're gone, my heart is amiss.
I see your face, if only in mist.
Someday we'll touch, hold hands once again.
And forever remember the way we began.

Love Dan
January 2019

Dealing with the Loss of My Loved Ones

My mother died just before my sixth birthday. I did not really know what happened at that time (I later found out she had died in the 1953 flu epidemic). As young kids, my sister and I only knew we really missed our mother.

The night of her death, my dad was at work. Mommy slept with my three-year-old sister and I in our bedroom because her brother was visiting from Virginia and sleeping in her bed.

I'll never forget waking up early that morning and seeing Mom lying in a strange position across another bed in our room. I called to her then got up, went to her, and saw she was very still. Her eyes were open, and she had blood coming out of her mouth down her cheek. I, along with my sister, and with increasing anxiety, kept trying to wake her up.

I don't remember, but I'm sure we started crying and pleading loud enough so that Mom's brother heard us and came in to see what was going on (thank the Lord he was there).

I remember he put me and Debbie in the living room and told us to wait there. Mommy was sick. He then called my aunt and uncle who came rushing over from their house. In the bedroom, there was a lot of whispering and what sounded like crying. They then took me to my Aunt Lizzie's home where I stayed that day. I remember feeling sad and lonely and not quite knowing why. I knew something happened to my mother, but I really didn't understand what was going on.

Later, I remember being at her funeral in Bluefield. Of course, Debbie and I were told that Mommy was now in Heaven.

At that time, I think I still believed Mom would be back when she got well.

At the funeral, I was seated with my Aunt Lizzie and Uncle Basil.

I remember two of my uncles slowly walking with Dad into the funeral home, holding onto his arm. Somewhere before he got to the front, he literally collapsed in tears. Then I remember they helped him leave. I don't think I saw my dad for a few days after that.

Let's move to a time sixty-six years later.

It was the summer of 2018. Valerie, my wife, had been complaining about her stomach hurting. Sometime in August, she had a doctor's appointment. They saw something and decided they needed to immediately perform an operation.

At this time, Valerie and I had been married over fifty years. We had three wonderful children and were planning on enjoying our retirement years.

Then it happened.

When they operated, the doctors discovered cancer in her stomach and took out all they could. Apparently, they got most of it except for one little spot that they told us could be eradicated with radiation.

In late September, Valerie began radiation treatments. After each weekly treatment, she had to go home and rest for a couple of days. That fall and early winter, she and I spent much time talking about our lives, our children, our hopes, serious things, wonderful things, and continued to build on our very deep relationship.

I realized more and more each day how much I loved her.

At this time, the kids became worried about their mom. Although living away from home, they were spending more and more time with us. They a wanted to be close to Mom.

It turned out; the radiation treatments were not successful. Although, I refused to believe they weren't. (I do remember we met a lady in the lab waiting room who was also undergoing radiation. A couple of weeks into the program, we did not see her. When we asked, the receptionist said she had passed away.) I did not believe it would happen to Valerie. Still, around Christmas, we found out there was nothing more that radiation could do. So, to her relief, Valerie quit going.

Around the first of January, she was especially sick. I took her to the emergency room. After a few hours and some medication, they let her go home.

Now, I'll approach this story in a different manor.

Valerie and I love the Lord. He has been the strength of our marriage. We had some hard times, some interpersonal struggles, and some physical and financial setbacks. But our trust in God and our love for each other never wavered. Although, my dedication to Him sometimes did. We always believed that He would help us through those rocky times.

Now, that She was so sick, I still had my whole trust in Him. I believed He would heal her. I believed we both would be well upon this earth for years to come. Never dreaming as to what would soon happen.

In the last week of January, Valerie again had to be taken to the emergency room. This time, they admitted her to the hospital. She was really sick. I stayed with her that night and the next day, leaning close, praying for her, and holding her hand most of the time. That evening, the nursing staff and the doctors met with the family and I to talk about what was going on. They didn't give us a time, but they did say it could be soon. At that moment, I became numb. I couldn't believe something like this was happening.

Then, a great peace came over me. If something did happen, she definitely would be in Heaven and without pain. Yeah, but I would miss her. The numbness remained.

That night, the kids told me to go home and sleep. I had been up for forty-eight plus hours. Reluctantly, I did as they requested. Michelle spent the night with Mom.

Early the next day, I was back in Valerie's intensive care room. That morning, the nurses then moved her to another room. A little later, I discovered why. This was to be Valerie's final in-hospital move.

Sometime around noon, with her family gathered around, a unique lady came into the room and played beautiful harp music. With her harp, she created a peaceful, reverent atmosphere in the room. It seemed a holy atmosphere. The family was crying. I kept holding Valerie's hand, and Valerie seemed at peace as she smiled with her eyes closed.

To my amazement, I then saw something I couldn't believe. Her mouth opened, and just above her head I saw a flicker of something rise up. I don't know what it was, but I know I saw it. I want to believe it was her soul leaving her body.

Then I realized Val was home.

I entered a state of shock and denial. I could not believe she had left me after nearly fifty-one years. And yet, I was still comforted, realizing where she went at. Literally, no more pain.

Then, for some reason, I thought about her being with her mom and dad and also, with my dad.

And for the first time ever, she was meeting my mommy! That, folks, is a glorious thought! What hope! What comfort! Through the funeral, through the burial, I was in a state of shock. I then started to realize that worldly things did not matter anymore; possessions, belongings, things, places, finances, "worldly treasures." Nothing was important except my wife and my relationship with God.

In Him is my treasure, in Him is my resource, in Him is my hope.

Oh yes, I was sad. Oh yes, I missed my wife. But I was also assured that our separation wouldn't be forever.

The only thing, though, was I did not like being alone. I did not like being the odd person in couple's outings. I was very uncomfortable being alone in a big house, the only person in my car, the only person shopping for groceries, sitting by myself in church, coming home from church by myself, eating alone ... I sorely missed Valerie.

A week or so after Valerie passed, I received a condolence message from an old friend. Someone I grew up with, so to speak. We went to the same church, the same class at school, lived in the same town, had the same beliefs.

I was really warmed by what she said in her note. So, I wrote her back and thanked her for being so sincere. I knew she was a good Christian from our old days, and from what I picked up on the internet, I knew she and her husband had been missionaries, founded churches, and pastored numerous churches for over forty-six years. I also knew that her husband had passed away a couple months before Val.

I wrote her back and a little exchange began.

As I said, I was lonely. Val and I had a good marriage. We loved and respected each other.

We enjoyed each other; God was in our marriage!

When she passed away, my personal world collapsed. Now, all I could do was rely on God.

So, my prayer was: *God, you're in charge of my life, I gave... I give my life to you. Please use me.*

Bonnie and I wrote more. I noticed couples in the church holding hands, so I started writing poetry. (*Soon to be published*).

One thing I would like to say is that Val and I had a good marriage. Of course, I did not want to let that end. But I was still on earth. Val was in Heaven.

I worshipped God, and I knew He did not want me to be lonely.

I've heard it said that couples with good marriages tend to get remarried faster. My kids did not understand, and it was hard to explain. My companion, my nearest friend, my wife, was gone. I hope they will not have to go through what I, and Bonnie, went through.

I know God led me to Bonnie and her to me. I truly believe our getting together was a result of our cry to God. We truly do love each other.

As we got closer, we realized we could really talk to each other. We really spoke the same language. Spiritually, theologically, socially, and, of course, culturally. We liked the same things; we talked the same language. We were both raised in low-income families. We discovered that if we wanted anything during our teen years, we had to earn our own money. We both loved the Lord and spent much of our youth in and around church. We were friends and had many mutual friends. We really liked each other during our growing up years (I always did look up to Bonnie), but, weirdly enough, we never dated. Yeah, we were involved together in many youth activities. But we never dated.

Upon high school graduation, I went into the Air Force, and she went to college. We went our separate ways for more than fifty years, just like God wanted.

What a life we both lived. Living to serve God, and living to serve our families.

Now, look where we are. Together. Until God again calls one of us home.

(Our relationship and courtship is another story. And it's a goodn'.)

God's Amazing Blessing

Bonnie and Me

You know our love just shouldn't be.
I mean this thing between you and me.
We had our lives all planned out.
Married the right persons without a doubt.

You had your home, I had mine.
Seems we both had a wonderful time.
Then life happened, we weren't prepared.
Too young we say, and we were scared.

How would we live in our newfound life?
Tragic and sad, I lost my wife.
You were so strong, helping your man.
Can we ever be normal again?

We could not guess the tragic we share.
Planning a future no longer there.
A miracle of miracles, I know it to be.
I found you, and you found me.

Now there's hope, a brand-new promise.
A faith and love, that grows among us.
We're not sure, what the future holds.
We live as we can till, we grow old.

Never again will I take for granted
the life I have, not for a minute.
I only know God has the plan.
All we can do is what we can.

Only He knows for us what's best.
Occasionally, we know He gives a test.
Finally, my life, I offer to you.
That's all I have till my Life is thru.

My love for you is growing.

You're Becoming a Habit

I love talking to you. You're peaceful in the
storms of life.
I couldn't believe we talked an hour and a half.
Last night. Went too fast.
You're becoming a habit!
Wait a minute. (That could be my next poem title.)
Will work on it. WAIT A MINUTE ...
...Worked on it ...!

You're Becoming a Habit!

You're becoming a habit!
Love hearing you speak.
Imagine how life would be
with you here next to me.

Want to hear you talk.
Your message soothes my soul.
You understand my wanting
to be under your control.

You bring life to the hopeless.
You bring hope to my life.
I'm learning to need your voice
to whisper away my strife.

We could make a marvelous team.
Conquer our world that remains,
fill whatever's left of our time
with a message of our love exchanged.

I love when we're together,
even if only through our voice.
You stimulate my longing,
to make some caressing choice.

I'm hoping my yearning happens.
I'm happy when I Hope
that our life can be together.
Dear God, please take control.

Oh Dear, look what you made me do.

Call me Anytime

❖

Anytime you want to call me,
anytime you're feeling low,
anytime you're thinking of me
with anything you want me to know.
That's the time I want to hear you.
Just your voice will be enough.
For there's times when I am lonely,
and what you say will build me up.

How Long Has This Gone On?
60 years!

Poetry Contest

Wish I could see your smile,
the glint of sun in your hair.
Make you more than a dream,
Bonnie Jean.

Wish I could feel your hands so soft,
your presence so near,
your voice so clear,
Bonnie Jean.

Wish I could feel your lips on mine
as our hearts entwine.
That would be fine,
Bonnie Jean.

Wish we could stand
hand in hand, with a plan.
Oh, how my heart would beam,
Bonnie Jean.

Better verses are written, I'm sure.
But non as pure
as my growing love of you,
Bonnie Jean.

That God Has a Plan with Us In His Mind

Although we met so long ago,
we are strangers now, getting to know.
What we missed, in our separate lives,
the trails we blazed, the paths we tried.

We are now lost, wanting to find,
a new direction with each other in mind.
So many years have passed us by;
we'll feel defeated if we don't try.

To cross that gap, create our new world.
Decide if it's late to give it a whirl.
Bonnie, it's you, and it could be I.
Who makes a move to reach for our sky?

Years have passed, and maybe our youth,
but in our hearts we will know the truth.
Our Bodies have changed, but not the wish,
of living again until we are dismissed.

May God bless our efforts and protect as we try
to regain our lives before we must die.
Our time is now hectic as trials unfold,
things to get right with mysteries untold.

Remind us of times when we first started.
Our life yet lived, our roads yet charted.
Don't know, Bonnie, if it will turn out,
but I'm hoping as we talk, we can both Shout.

That God has a plan with us in His mind.

You Know What I Miss

Bonnie: You know what I miss? Holding Hands!
In church yesterday, a couple was standing in front of me singing and holding hands.
I felt so lonely. Val and I held hands all of the time. She was a good hand holder.
We'd even walk through the house holding hands.
Don't even mention walking down the street or in the grocery store.
And I miss pinches and touching. Not hurting pinches, just little bumps to let me know she was there, and rubs, you know the kind, just walking up and rubbing by me.
And hugs, boy, do I miss hugs! Surprise hugs from the back, a reach over and squeeze while standing in church, a morning hug, a hug for no reason at all, and leg squeezing while setting in a restaurant, and oh yes, those thigh bumps. Of course, the kisses, and cuddling, and boy, do I miss those hugs.
I wonder, will those "little things," those "love touches," ever happen again?
Maybe with you? Who knows?

Love Danny

Another Of My "Edgy" Thoughts

Ok, hang on. I'm in a poetic mood. Don't be too scared.
Poetry doesn't have to rhyme!
True poetry elicits a feeling in the mind of the reader.
Let's see if this works.

Can you see walking into church
Mr. and Mrs.
Can you enjoy long car rides
Mr. and Mrs.
Can you envision getting a hug anytime
you need one
Mr. and Mrs.
Can you smell trees when walking through
the forest
Mr. and Mrs.
Can you feel warmth going to the grocery store
Mr. and Mrs.
Can you believe telling our friends
Mr. and Mrs.
Can you hear the laughter walking through our
front door
Mr. and Mrs.
Can you understand who really controls the family
Mrs. and Mr.
Can you imagine being introduced as
Mr. and Mrs.
Will You Look With Me?

Oh, I Hope It's Yes

Don't like being alone.
Can't stand the pace.
Miss your lovely presence.
Would love your warm embrace.

Try to live without you,
lonely is all I get.
Need your smile, your smell,
if only a little bit.

As I sat here moping,
crying in my tears,
feeling sorry for that guy
I keep seeing in the mirror.

You are bright like sunshine,
driving back clouds of pain
with your aura of sweetness,
like a freshness after a rain.

Can we do it forever?
Hold each other tight,
calling each other sweet things
late into the night.

As I write this message,
I wonder what it will be.
Will I look back and wonder?
Or will you look back with me?

Will side by side be we,
Facing our future together?
Oh, I hope it's yes.
There nothing can be better.

Something to Pray About Today

———————◦———————

I am more than enthralled because of who you are
and what you mean to me.
I'm dreaming of what our life could be like if we
were together.

I can see fragrant rose petals under your feet
every morning.

A mist of fresh sunshine in your hair every day.

I can see your beautiful smile spreading cheer and
gentle warmth to all you meet.

I can hear your soft voice cradling the hearer with
melodious encouragement and warmth.

I can feel the touch of your graceful hands in mine
and feel the embrace of your loving
arms around my shoulders.

Bonnie, I really do know you're more than special,
and I'm praying that God will quickly reveal to us
His plan for our lives. Oh, that there will be some-
thing that conclusively proves to
us both that as a couple,
He will use us for His Kingdom.

Everything to this moment seems such a blessed
miracle. How we talked, how we remembered, how

we felt, how we supported, how we comforted,
how we dreamed.
Now, we must pray and wait to see what the
Lord has in store for us.
Bonnie, what an exciting, important
day June 5th will be.

Gotta Get Over This ...
Wait a Minute ... Don't Wanna!

———◆———

I'm wanting to talk/communicate with you
constantly.
I can't seem to get you out of my mind.
The word is *pining*.
Bonnie, I continually pine for you.
Well, maybe not that far yet.
But really close to it.
(I just looked up pining in the dictionary.)
And still I know my pining (second meaning/defini-
tion) is because you are a wonderful mystery to me.
I really think you always were.
I wonder if God is now working things out in our
lives so we can enjoy and
support each other at this time?

Now, if you can figure out what I just said,
then would you please tell me?
I believe if I told you in the most simplistic terms
of how much
I care for you. They would be:
I need you; I want you; I want to hold your hand.
(That's familiar)
I could probably get the message over.
And trying to be simple is very complicated.
Bonnie, I can't get you out of my mind!
Love, Hugs, Kisses, Danny

Oh, To Sit In Church Someday

Oh, to sit in church someday.
Hold your soft hand, warm in mine.
Feeling days when we were young,
knowing that our thoughts entwine.

Sitting in church, a wonderful thing.
What better than awakening love,
realizing we both honor our King,
feeling His love down from above

Will we ever, it seems a must,
that someday, I'll feel your touch.
Then my heart will flutter in song.
Romantic words to you belong

Will I ever feel your touch,
feel your spirit, see your face,
hold your hand, sitting in Church
while we sing Amazing Grace.

June 2019

Bonnie and the Red Ford Truck

Come along with me, Bonnie,
for a wonderful ride in my truck.
On a mountain road we'll go,
looking for a big deer buck.

She's old, she rattles, she's tattered.
But her heart is big and strong.
Get in her, feel the fun
as we go riding along.

Maybe down to the seashore.
I promise the ride won't be boring.
We'll see the breakers, the famous waves,
and see the seagulls soaring.

We'll bounce along, singing our song
side by side in my big, red Ford.
It could be yours if you desire.
Something to take to the store.

Just like the olden days
when a boy and his favorite girl
rode high in a big, red Ford.
and together they planned their world.

2019 A funny for Bonnie

Good Morning, Sweet Bonnie

———◦———

I really do hope you have an absolutely awesome, amazing day today. Excuse me for being so blunt, but I really believe you deserve many positive, wonderful days in your life. I'm praying this one will be filled with a wonderful adventure. May it be a relaxing, fun time with your relatives. May you come home safe, tired, and yet energized for whatever is next in your life.

One of the things I want to do with you is to take you to fun and interesting places.

Also, to quiet and romantic places where we can talk, hold hands, and simply cuddle.

By the way, sometimes I read what I write and am really embarrassed. I know I can really be forward, and I apologize if I offend you.

However, Bonnie, I know you are very special, and there is no one else I would rather be forward with. Strange, we haven't seen each other in years and yet, I know you, and I know who you are. I also know we'll discover just how compatible we are on June 5th.

I'm waiting for the moment we first meet. I'm wondering just how it will be? I can visualize the world slowing down like in the movies. And in slow motion, we reach out, touch each other, and you will fall into my arms. I know I'll let out a gasp. And there may even be a tear of happiness in my eye. There definitely will be laughter in my heart, and a stuttering in my voice.

Bonnie, I'm Living For That Day!

Yes, Beautiful, but I'd rather see
the charms of your face!
The warmth of your smile,
the touch of your hand,
the whisper of your words,
the smell of your hair,
the softness of your lips,
the wisdom of your wit,
the brightness of you glance,
the song of your voice,
the cuddle of your arms,
the grace of your walk,
the happiness in your laugh.
Oh, yes, and you, you, you.

Leaving On a Jet Plane

Ten minutes ago, I missed you.
Now, even more.
An hour from now will be terrible
as I wait at the departure door.

No plane yet, wonder why?
Keep looking upward,
hoping to fly.
Ah-ha, here comes one.
Slowly Taxing, could it be?
No, this one's not for me!

Finally, my plane. Two days late.
Who's to blame? Could be fate.
Got another day. A pleasant surprise.
More holding hands, looks into your eyes.

Now I've gone on another great plane,
more lonesome than ever, only memories remain.
Tell your family I love them, they're a plea-
sure to know.
You raised them well. Their upbringing really shows.
Would have stayed if I could, but must return west.
Things to do, people to see, before we can rest.

Bonniefire

I just saw your Back Porch Bonniefire.

Very impressive. Hope you had a fire hydrant close
at hand, or at least a bucket of water! You know how
to build a fire. Wait a minute. You're a country girl,
and country girls know their fire. I'll bet you
had that under control the whole time.
Except for that oo-nn-ee little second
when you took this picture.

Anyway, good job country girl! Did the rest of the
family enjoy your burgers? Would love to have one
right now. No, I'd much rather have you right now. I
really miss you. I'm thinking back and really realize
how much I enjoyed that picnic at the park. What
wonderful memories I have with you.

I Miss You

Handholding in the park.
Walking together in the dark.
Enjoying our time of reverie.
Nobody around but you and me.

Watching the moon over the trees.
Feeling the warm summer breeze.
Smelling the damp at Gatewood Park.
Strolling the aisles of ol' Walmart.

Couldn't have a better time.
I am yours and you are mine.
Having to dodge your famous pothole.
Remembering to turn so must go slow.

Bonnie, this trip meant much to me.
It seemed your presence set me free.
Lunch In Wytheville was so much fun,
and driving home, boy, what a run!

Up to Bluefield to see the folks.
They all love you, that's no joke.
Donna, Joe Lenny, and Linda,
they all love you, especially Aunt Lizzie.

Trips to Radford, Roanoke, and Draper.
Up to your cabin, boy, what a caper!
Loved the place, can really see why.
Must have been hard when you all said goodbye.

Finally, the plane. A new story began.
Up and back, and up again.
A comedy of errors, but I didn't care.
Just mention more days to spend with you there.

Now, I miss you with all of my heart.
Next time we meet, let's never part.
My love for you was born from sadness.
My love for you is now filled with gladness.

Ok, it's heartache time, waiting to see
when I can love you and you can love me.
Permission takes time, hurdles to cross.

Love, Danny

Errors and Omissions

Have you noticed lately that it seems nobody is at fault? Or it's someone else's fault; or the psycho-social environment is at fault; or the parents are at fault; or the authorities are at fault because they are the authorities; or no one is at fault, especially if they don't inhale.

Never, never, never will you hear such obligation equivocation words for any possible errors or omissions within the pages of this publication. When I make a mistake, I admit it. If you find an error, I'll be first to say it's my fault.

To show you how well I can deal with mistakes, I want to apologize in advance for any possible errors or omissions that you may have found.

Of course, I've done everything possible to eradicate all mistakes. I've proofread everything more than once, I've double checked with English teachers, I let my wife read it, I've made phone calls, I ran the spell check, "I" even let "me" touch it. I don't want to be blamed for anything that is not my fault.

However, if there is a mistake in this publication, I just wanted you to know that it was 100% correct when it left my office. Any errors or omissions that it may contain occurred somewhere in the Post Office.

See how easy it is for me to admit my faults.

Dan French
Head of errors and omissions redacting department

CPSIA information can be obtained
at www.ICGtesting.com
Printed in the USA
LVHW071928130422
716130LV00019B/549